THE DIRTY BUSINESS

TOM SCOTT

OTHER BOOKS BY TOM SCOTT

Verse
Seeven Poems by Maister Francis Villon
>> *Pound Press, Tunbridge Wells, 1953*
An Ode til New Jerusalem
>> *M. MacDonald, Edinburgh, 1956.*
The Ship and Ither Poems
>> *Oxford University Press, London and New York, 1963*
At the Shrine o the Unkent Sodger
>> *Akros Publications, Preston, Lancs., 1968*
Brand the Builder
>> *Ember Press, London, 1975*
The Tree
>> *Borderline Press, 1977*

Prose
Dunbar: A Critical Exposition
>> *Oliver & Boyd, Edinburgh, 1966.*
>> *Barnes and Noble, New York, 1966.*
>> *Greenwood Press, Westport, Connecticut, 1977.*
Tales of King Robert the Bruce
>> *Pergamon Press, Oxford, 1969.*
>> *Gordon Wright Publishing, Edinburgh 1975.*
Tales of Sir William Wallace
>> *Gordon Wright Publishing, Edinburgh, 1981.*

Edited
Oxford Book of Scottish Verse (with John MacQueen)
>> *Clarendon Press, Oxford, 1966 et seq.*
Late Medieval Scots Poetry
>> *Heinemann, London, 1967.*
>> *Barnes and Noble, New York, 1967.*
Penguin Book of Scottish Verse
>> *Penguin Books, London, 1970 et seq.*

THE DIRTY BUSINESS

A Poem About War

Tom Scott

The Blew Blanket Library,
Luath Press, Ltd.

First Edition: 1986

INTRODUCTION

We must think people, not statistics.

That is a quotation — the key line — from the following poem.   Milton said of poetry that it is *'less subtle and fine, but more simple, sensuous and passionate'* than prose.   To me, this means that it is more human, personal, warm-blooded.   Those military minds which can think that winning some battle or other is worth the expense of, say, a hundred thousand 'casualties' are not thinking in terms of their own wives, children and friends.   They are not thinking of people at all, but of counters, figures, chess-men.   But to me, a simple human being of sensibility and passion, they are flesh and blood — my flesh and blood, no matter what their nationality or degree of guilt.   I was twenty-one when the Global War broke out in 1939; I was twenty-seven when it ended, and to me the war was largely a matter of what people were doing to each other, or what the machine they had created was doing to them.   Yet I took sides, had to take sides, 'defend the bad against the worse'; hoping the better would emerge from the holocaust.

Poetry being essentially a celebration of life, is it possible to make poetry out of insane destruction of life?   Out of war?   Yes, for poetry is also criticism of anti-life phenomena in society.   And there is the traditional war-poetry of the epic fathers of poetry: there is the

I

Iliad and there is the *Aeneid*, and so much later poetry down to Owen, Rosenberg and others in this century. Such epic-type poetry is the background to *The Dirty Business,* a poetry of historical events, not the lyric 'gems' of Palgrave's Golden Treasury.

In war-poetry imagination drinks deep of facts — not always the most poetical of material, however passionately felt. But explicit factuality, however condensed (a main function of verse — hence its memorability), is to the work as bone is to flesh. Incredible though it is to those of us who lived through the Global War, to later generations it will become as vague and distant as the Napoleonic War was to ours. Who would bother to look up the history books for the background to a work of verse? Therefore the work must contain, however inadequately, an outline of its own context. And of those historians who will be most aware of that inadequacy, the errors inevitably creeping in, I crave indulgence. This is a poem about a piece of history; in no sense a historical work. I have nowhere knowingly distorted or bent history to my purpose, but have stuck as close as I could to my many sources in book form. My interpretations of the facts are of course my own.

The *personae* in the poem, from the line quoted as title to this note on, are mainly imaginary, though founded on real people; but occasionally the real names are used. I myself as narrator speak in different masks and moods: the soldier who opens the work; my proper self; the mood of war itself, with its drive, battle-rage, determination, endurance beyond endurance, will to win, unbelievable (perverse?) courage of all combatants without which it could never have been carried out, in Section I; the speculative observer; the involved sufferer whose outraged sensibility makes the whole a cry of agony. Finally, the Adam-Eve *persona* as the archetypical human race itself, the species *homo sapiens* which so far has survived the horrendous atrocity of war, that erstwhile game of a lop-sided patriarchal society careering to its own destruction and that of all animal species, in nuclear genosuicide which, though the outcome of

II

war, will in no sense be a 'war'. A 'war' always has a winner and a loser. No action which has only losers can be called a war. Therefore there is no such thing as nuclear 'war'. But, as Adam-Eve see, there is still hope. There can be faith and charity. There can be Peace on Earth. Humankind can still inherit the Earth, and deserve to inherit it. But only if the lessons our gift of hindsight can learn from history are in fact grasped, digested, and lead to a change of will from destruction to creation.

Tom Scott

THE DIRTY BUSINESS

War's a damn dirty business.
Here's this skeery Frau on at me
about some Ivan eftir her dochter.
Whit the hell can I dae?   Nane o my business.
Whit did the Germans dae in Russia?
Naebody's war is cushy.

Miners get their bodies dirty,
sodgers their sauls.........

Where are the war poets? cried the whores of the press.
Can a dirty business have its poetry?
The poetry of war is in the pity, said Owen,
whose fierce compassion burns in his every line.
Like Rosenburg and other poet-martyrs
he bore his personal witness and passed on.
But the challenge is to understand.
The poetry is in the understanding.

1

Where did it begin?   This dirty business
began for us in the hell of the trenches,
the Kaiser's war to avoid a civil war
followed by the vengeance of Versailles
leading to Hitler, the Versailles-maddened bull.
And it began with the Russian revolution
that set the the capitalist world a-tremble,
conscious of its *mene tekhel upharsin,*
and fearing Stalin more than Hitler.

The otter is born to kill the eel,
the wolf to prey on the fawn, the weasel
on the rabbit, the fox upon the pheasant,
the frog to eat the may-fly, the heron the frog.
the strong prey on the weak, the stronger on the strong.

Think of nature, and we think
of human nature, not bound by instinct,
free to season impulse with reason.
Think of species, and we think
of the human species, destined
to inherit earth as one community.
Think of that, and Marx steps in
to talk of technique, motives of greed and profit
not compatible with social harmony.
And behind Marx the whole Judaic witness
from Abraham to Yeshu, the God of love
for neighbour as for self,
the law of our species.

Freud and Jung would point to hidden factors
deep in the psyche; and in Deutschland, Lawrence saw
the old Wotan rouse and take the road
to the east, and his own destruction.

Hitler never understood the role he played
in Churchill's psyche, his Moby Dick
to Churchill's Ahab; how, far beyond conscious cause,
Churchill saw in him Incarnate Evil,
and set that bulldog will on its destruction,
a personal, invincible hate
that could have no end
but the death of one or both.

Churchill was set to kill his shadow, Hitler.

Each piece on the board some million lives,
the dirty business seems a game of chess
played with enthusiasm by born Masters
who never themselves, normally, spill their blood,
though they play till the last drop of everyone else's.

Hitler, Hirohito, Mussolini:
Churchill, Roosevelt, Stalin:
three-a-side chess between the governors
played with the expendable lives of the governed.
This time the winners changed the rules,
Hitler and Mussolini lost their lives,
Tojo was hanged for his master, Hirohito,
as that peacock MacArthur sought to use him
in the capitalist gang-up against the Soviet Union.
Lesser leaders too were done to death
for what were deemed 'war crimes' —
going beyond where cricketing gentlemen go.
But what greater war crimes were committed
than Dresden, Tokyo, Hiroshima, Nagasaki?

If criminal laws are founded on Moral Law
the whole war was the worst crime yet committed.

Intelligence, like a machine, is morally neutral,
no better, no worse, than the person using it.
What worth a high I.Q. in a murderer's soul
Or high I.Qs in a spiv society
ruled by the values of the (black) market
where everything has its price
and nothing its value?

The better his brain, the worse the criminal.

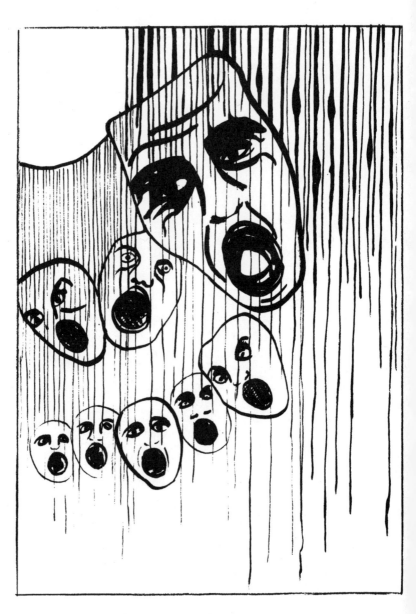

It is the cause, my soul.....The cause is us,
that we must murder innocence.
Let annalists and analyists discuss
the causes, as they must, the cause is us.
Other species fight, but they don't wage war.

There was of course Hitler and the German bourgeoisie
reacting in terror at sight of the abyss
the crash of capitalism opened under them,
dread of wage-slave rebellion, fear of their vengeance,
of communism, dread of the unknown.
Result — a national psychosis, all
the hell of the German soul erupting,
the course already clearly plotted in *Mein Kampf.*
Those of us not wilfully blind knew
what we faced, and knew the only way to stop it:
a pact by Britain and France with the USSR,
and any others willing, to contain the Germans
till the madness wore itself out on their own soil.
Even Churchill, no friend of socialism,
saw such a pact as the one hope for peace.
But the capitalist powers were more afraid
of socialism than of Nazi power,
their ranks full of pro-fascist gangsters
who, trying to ride the tiger, unleashed the war.
Our last chance, Munich, was missed.

Capitalism: moribund, obsolete, damned
by its own incompetence, its contradictions.
People starving because there was too much wealth:
food mountains rased because people couldn't afford food:
millions unemployed in a world short of labour:
figures in books worshipped as the idol Money,
money having long been displaced by credit:

under-consumption miscalled over-production:
Profit and Wages locked in unending battle.
The crash of the Wall Street gambling den
proved that capitalism is in its death-throes,
socialism its only living heir.

But the ruling-class countered the revolution.
Hitler was financed by millionaires
from all over Europe and the U.S.A.
eager to halt social evolution.

The dirty business that counter-revolution.

War in the Far East too could have been prevented
by a triple alliance of Russia, the U.S. and China
against Japan, with the Commonwealth abetting.
For many reasons it was not forthcoming:
isolationism, lack of vision,
of grasp of Japan's imperial ambition and might.

How many guessed that the image of Hirohito,
the quiet little introvert, the biologist
paddling about absorbed among his shellfish,
masked the tyrant who alone
ordered the attack on Pearl Harbor
against the advice of his experts and commanders?
Out of the fantasies of centuries broke
in Japan too a national psychosis,
the little man's dream of conquering the world.

Hirohito was master enough to survive,
his place on the scaffold taken by Tojo,
and survived MacArthur to make Japan
the third industrial power on Earth —
not by the samurai sword, but consumer goods.
Hitler and Hirohito, the chief war criminals,
escaped the scaffold where their minions died.
But while Hitler and all his works were swept out of sight
into the rubbish bin of time,
still the emperor rules Japan,
the spider lurking in the web centre,
still intent on world conquest.

Only Hitler and Hirohito
could have united in common cause

the British empire and the USSR,
France, China and the U.S.A.
What but their war would have reduced
the pre-war world of Kilkenny cats,
the rival gangs of capitalist nations,
to only two super-powers
and communist China?

The war was revolution in disguise.

Nature uses the scourge of war
to flog her pig-headed humans
along the road she's chosen,
the integration of the species
in a one-for-all and all-for-one world.

World War Two?   No,
the first was but European.   The dirty business
is the Global War, the World War One and only:
another would not be war but genosuicide.

My, and my generation's, lot it was
to grow up to meet the Global War grew up
to meet us, that robbed us of our youth
and too many of our lives.

    The cup my Father has prepared,
   shall I not drink it?

     Jim lost
in the Battle of Britain, Tam and Bob and John
shot from the skies, Ian killed in a plane crash,
Alex done to death in a Japanese prison camp,
Niven killed on the Normandy beaches,
      too many
from the musing wynds of old St. Andrews,
who used to haunt my dreams, my nightmares,
accusing, asking, pleading, demanding —
     what?

Report me and my cause aright?

Chamberlain, Halifax, names to abhor,
abetting, not appeasing, Hitler,
forcing surrender by Czechoslovakia,
willing to trade off parts of the empire
for peace with Hitler as France goes down,
their treason untold to the British people.
The Cabinet knew, but kept it secret.

Beware official secrecy.

After the crimes of the thirties, how could
Chamberlain declare war over Poland?
But so he did, and so it began.

Began for us piano-piano, *sotto voce,*
except for the war at sea,
Hitler reluctant to fight the Teuton English
whose ruling class preferred war with Russia.
But then came Narvik,
Denmark invaded, Norway,
the German fleet battered,
then Holland, Belgium and France.
The phoney war became real.

Snubbed by the allies, in Thirty-nine Stalin
despaired of the alliance might yet contain Hitler
and made a deal with the Nazi enemy.

No phoney war in Poland, cavalry
against armoured tank divisions,
torn apart by Hitler and Stalin.
No phoney war in Finland, Estonia,
Lithuania, Latvia, grabbed by Russia.

The Italian tyrant, a bumptious incompetent
soon to prove a ball and chain
round Hitler's ankles, struck first
at Albania, then Egypt and Greece.

No phoney war in the Far East
Nanking already raped by Japan,
an atrocious and sadistic orgy,
which set up the puppet Manchukuo.

One by one, around the Globe,
its war clamped its tentacles.

The real beginning, as we socialists knew,
was in Ethiopia, China, Spain:
the capitalists soft as butter on fascism,
hard as brass on socialism.
Among Tory M.P.s Churchill and Eden
almost alone in seeing Hitler
as a greater menace than Soviet Russia,
Nazism worse than Bolshevism,
a greater threat to the British empire.

> **Mao-tse-tung in China,**
> **Churchilll, Eden, Bevin, Attlee,**
> **Beaverbrook and others in Britain,**
> **Roosevelt in the U.S.A.**

all over the Globe were springing up
the men to meet humankind's enemies.

14

Wrapping the Earth in khaki and drill,
the loom of war weaves on, warp and woof,
up and down, from side to side.

The *Graf Spee* scuttled on the Rio Plata.

The British forces rescued from Dunkirk
as France goes under the jack-boot.

Britain closes the Burma Road,
batters Italian fleet at Taranto,
and again at Cape Matapan,
begins manoevres (why) in the desert.

Wavell shatters Mussolini's empire
in Africa, the emperor back in Abyssinia:
takes Tobruk and all north-east Africa.

Rommel replaces Italians in Tripoli,
puts British advances into reverse.

The Greek idiocy begins,
the British folly of Crete
a new Dardenelles but worse.

At first no U.S. involvement,
but Britain allowed cash and carry,
and U.S. forces take bases in Iceland.

Roosevelt re-elected a third term,
the Senate passes the Lend-Lease Bill
(the war proved the System's salvation?),
U.S. profiteers making a killing
unparalleled before or since —
the foundation of U.S. world domination.

The loom weaves endlessly on:
Greece, Yugoslavia, invaded,
Belgrade bombed nearly into the ground:
Rommel captures Tobruk.

Japan and Russia pledge neutrality.
The British are routed out of Crete
with horrific losses on both sides.
Cunningham's fleet so broken in the mess
U-boats control the Mediterranean,
Malta under atrocious air attack.
Wavell puts down 'revolt' in Syria.

Hitler, the whole of Europe under his heel,
snatches defeat from the jaws of victory
launching 'blitzkreig' on his Soviet ally.
Churchill welcomes 'that great warrior Stalin',
they sign a mutual assistance pact.

Japanese forces land in Indo-China.
The U.S. and Britain reply by imposing
embargo on raw materials to Japan,
tying a halter round Hirohito's neck.

While the Wehrmacht hurtles on to Rostow,
Churchill and Roosevelt draw up the Atlantic Charter,
Britain starts Arctic convoys to Russia,
Wavell, overworked by Churchill,
swops commands with Auchinleck —
a piece of folly soon regretted.

Tojo takes over as Japanese premier,
the loom weaves on and on.

Hirohito out-Hitlers Hitler
in self-destructive madness
by launching the attack on Pearl Harbour,
thus pulling down on his head
the one Pacific power could shatter Japan.

**Whom the gods wish to destroy, indeed
they first of all make mad.**

Hitler fails to take Moscow before the snows
and meets his nemesis, the Russian winter
as if Napoleon, the abler soldier,
had never suffered his Russian disaster.
And to crown himself king of fools,
he declares war on U.S.A.

Guam falls to Japan,
Wake and Hong Kong follow
and then Manila.
Burma is attacked,
then the Dutch East Indies.

The tentacles tighten round the whole Globe.

17

18

In Washington twenty-six nations
sign the United Nations Declaration,
a major victory for the revolution
underlying the dirty business.

In the desert Rommel routs Ritchie and Auchinleck,
Benghazi recaptured, or handed over:
Montgomery and Alexander replace them
and Rommel at last meets his betters.
El Alamein turns the war against him.

In Russia the agony drags on
the lives on both sides bleed in millions,
Timoshenko fails to hold the Crimea,
invincible winter punishing all.

Disaster spreads in the Pacific,
overpowered by the Japanese navy:
Rangoon is captured, Singapore follows,
Lashio and Mandalay.

Australia is shaken, Darwin bombed,
New Guinea attacked,
Batavia falls, Americans crushed and slaughtered in Bataan,
the Philippines taken, Corregidor.

But in the Coral Sea
The U.S. win the battle of Midway.

The Wehrmacht takes Sebastopol,
the Don Basin, Rostow,
lays seige to Stalingrad.

En una noche oscura..........
The blackout of the soul.

Labour unending
fighting and rending,
attacking, defending,
through the long night.

Sweating and bleeding,
rationed in feeding,
everything needing,
where is the light?

The Atlantic U-boat war drags on
but by May forty-three the Allies have won it.

U.S. marines take Guadacanal,
the Germans surrender at Stalingrad.

Wresting Burma from the Japanese,
Wingate crosses the river Chindwin.
Kursk and Rostow are recovered.

The U.S. Air Force, tipped off,
downs Yamomoto, Japan's best strategist:
everywhere the Axis in trouble.

Toiling on,
toiling on,
through the jungles, across the plain.
dragging on,
dragging on
through the snow or the rain.

Alexander takes Bizerta and Tunis,
the Italians and Germans surrender.
The Allies take over Sicily
and Mussolini is jailed by Badoglio.

The U.S. liberate New Guinea,
Mountbatten takes command in South-east Asia,
the Allies move into Calabria,
land at Salerno, the Germans take over
in Italy, Mussolini their puppet.

Climbing up,
Climbing up
up the treacherous mountain face,
slogging on,
slogging on,
all together in place.

The Russians retake Karkov, Smolensk,
Knepropetrovsk and Kiev,
the Italians take arms against the Germans,
U.S. Marines attack Bougainville.

The loom weaves on, filling the pattern.

Allied airmen hammer Germany,
bombing Berlin and other cities.

The Teheran conference comes and goes.

Russia takes Novgorod, the allies land
at Anzio, shell Monte Cassino,
the U.S. take many Pacific isles —
Eniwetok, Engeli, Kwajalein.
Hamburg is bombed near to destruction.

The Russians conquer Rumania,
re-take Minsk and Sebastopol,
Rome falls to the allies,
Free French seize Siena,
and Japan renews attacks on China.

June forty-four, the allies at last
open the second front in Normandy,
the mightiest invasion launched so far,
the Axis powers everywhere losing,
ferociously fighting each foot of the way.

> *We shall fight them at sea!*
> *We shall fight them on shore!*
>   *In the air.*
>   *Everywhere.*
>   *Everywhere?*
> *Yes, and put them all down!*

The Americans capture Cherbourg.
An attempt on Hitler's life fails.
As the Red Army nears the Vistula
Warsaw rises against the Germans
to hold Poland for the London government,
so Stalin leaves them to die,
as they do in their thousands, Warsaw rased.

Battling on, on, on, on!
Driving on, on, on, on!
Van to van.
Man to man.
If we can?
Till we win, win, win, win!

Saipan falls to the U.S.A.
Guam follows, Tojo resigns,
Tinian too is taken.

Paris is rescued from the Nazis,
Brussels, Antwerp (still intact).
The Arnhem shambles is perpetrated,
Bucharest falls to the Russians,
Athens to the British, Belgrade to Tito.

We cross the Rhine and the German borders.

Nowhere is it a country ramble
but blood, sweat, toil and tears.

We shall fight, fight, fight, fight!
We shall kill, kill, kill, kill!
We'll prevail.
We'll prevail.
We'll prevail?
Yes, or die, die, die, die.

23

24

The Killing.   The chess men really die,
are slain, slaughtered, murder each other
by the hundreds of thousands, real blood,
as the chess players order them to.

In the Philippines, in Leyte Gulf,
Luzon, Iwo Jima, and Okinawa
the Japanese fight to the death,
men, women, children, suicide
of whole communities by the emperor's will,
Bushido death, these and all
the American dead and wounded
stun the sentient mind,
freeze the sentient heart.

Our prodigal race lays waste its own.
How many Japanese should die,
the emperor wonders, to save his face?
To give Japan excuse for surrender?
'The emperor, in his infinite mercy,
having regard to the sufferings of his people......'
In Saipan they jump from cliffs
onto rocks, or to drown in the sea,
men throwing their wives and children
first, then leaping after them.

Warsaw 'liberated' by the Russians,
Dresden bombed into criminal history
by horrendous Harris, Budapest
surrenders to the Russians,
still the loom clatters on.

Yalta comes and goes.

In April nineteen forty-five
the U.S. — the world — loses its president.
Roosevelt, the great sea eagle, dies.
We haven't had a president since.

One more year of F.D.R.
and we'd all have been spared the atomic crime.
Yet the fools prattle that
'No man is irreplaceable'.

Rome had only the one Augustus.

German towns fall to the allies,
Belsen and Buchenwald burst
upon an incredulous world, Vienna
falls to the Russians, Mussolini
and his mistress killed by partisans,
the bodies hung upside down from cleeks.

The Germans surrender at Caserta.

Hitler shoots himself, Eva takes poison
and both their bodies are burned with petrol.

The Red Army captures Berlin.

The Potsdam conference comes and goes,
Churchill springs a victory election
and is swept from power in a Labour landslide,
Attlee in office with a socialist mandate.
The revolution discards the mask of war.

Rangoon is retaken, Okinawa
falls to the U.S. after sickening carnage.

26

From Tinian flies out a bomber
which commits Hiroshima.
Three days later comes Nagasaki.

Man, made in the image of God.

Gradually the loom falls silent.
The tentacles relax their grasp.
The chess players review their game.

The capitalist countries can now go back
to their normal wallow in commercial ordure
from the socialism enforced by war.

The dirty business is over.

The dirty business is over?

Statistics can give you the facts and figures,
the fifty million dead,
ours and theirs, as the chess players calculate,
so many Russians, so many Poles,
so many Germans, so many Jews,
Dutch, French, Belgians, Norwegians,
Danes, Italians, Greeks, Yugoslavs,
Czechs, Rumanians, Finns, Hungarians,
Japanese, Chinese, Malayans, Javans,
Burmese, Indians, Philippinos, Sumatrans,
British, Americans, Canadians, Australians,
New Zealanders, etc. — nearly all nations.
Figures are so tidy.   Neat book-keeping.

But figures have no blood to flow,
are not living persons,
sons and daughters of their fathers' loins,
their mothers' wombs, flesh of our flesh,
bone of our bone, whatever the skin.
'Make you go cut we, we no go bleed
same like white man, hu-uh?'
Members all of the human family,
members one of another,
fifty million human worlds,
a nightful of throbbing stars.
It was the living flesh that died,
not figures we mourn but the living names,
we who are still here to mourn,
who live in the shadow of total extinction.

We must think people, not statistics.

Think that yae nicht bombs faa
(Scotland aye thirled to the English Treasury)
on unlikely Glesca, hooses turn rubble
and in the rubble Maisie deid,
wee Tosh in her airms,
Jean and Alan beside her deid.
But Bill, in his barracks at Perth
lives to come hame to bury his loves,
syne gaes back ti the war.   Back?   The war
is aa aroond us, follaes us like oor shadow.

Multiply that by a million, add
atrocities and depths of dehumanization
unimaginable but true
in every area of the Earth
and you get some notion
beyond sensibility
of the unprecedented, machine-wrought agony
the dirty business perpetrated.
Not Owen's compassion could encompass it,
nor could Dante's, for Hell
was only for sinners — so-called by Aquinas —
while war is for innocent victims.

August nineteen forty, on Cupar station
I mysel met gunner Jimmy, juist twinty-wan,
a fairmer's son oot Strathtyrum wey,
the yae survivor o his air force intake,
on his wey back for the last time
ti the Battle o Britain.
Ye can sense the dreid
under the daethly calm.

Churchill rises one night from dinner,
phones Colonel Nicholson in Calais:
to help the Dunkirk rescue, Calais
must be held to the last man.   It is.

At Saint-Nazaire, the Lancastria
blown up, the night ablaze
with the sea of burning oil
and Davie Broun frae Leuchars ane
o three thousand broiled in that inferno.
Churchill hid it from the British people.

Ma ficca gli occhi a valle......

But fix your eyes on the vale: draws near
that tide of blood within the which there boil
those who violently harm their neighbours......

And in the desert
Sorley proves himself again
a Gael of the heroic age,
while George, surviving the desert war
is driven mad by fascists in Greece.
Garioch taken prisoner, muses
pent up at night behind the wire,
on how the self-same stars he sees
look down on his Peg in Edinburgh.

Him Japanee, he velly funny man!
Small boy, he lun down stleet,
Him Japanee take bayonet,
cut all up belly!   I laugh!
Him Japanee velly funny man!
— our carpenter aboard the Hai Lee.

Little Spring Flower, aged thirteen,
father and mother used for bayonet practice,
the bayonet cheaper than the bullet
(they learned it from the Cameron Highlanders?)
stripped and tied on a bed, raped
by forty-three Japs, queuing at the door,
left there for casual use
and then the juddering, gibbering wreck
bayoneted to death.

Just an old Samurai custom?

Chinese and other babies tossed
from bayonet to bayonet,
people buried up to their necks,
men cloven to demonstrate
that the samurai sword can't REALLY
split a man from head to crotch.

Achilles groaned and wept for Patroclus dead,
then took up his war-gear and went to seek Hector.
War a noble game for Greek heroes.

Marilka, Daddy's pet, in Auschwitz
reduced to skin and bone, one day
stoops to pick up potato peelings.

Strapped to the flogging block in public
against regulations her backside bared
takes twenty-five measured strokes of the whip,
and each time she faints in soused with water
until she comes round, then the torture goes on.
Zwanzig. Einundzwanzig. Zweiundzwanzig.
Later, in London, in the room above me
where Tadek nightly caresses her scars,
her screams on the block whiles tear the night.

Nothing I find in Darwin, Marx or Jung
accounts for the ubiquitous fact
of humankind's ferocity to its own,
the unplumbed depths of cruelty
humans plunge each other into —
Man, the most ferocious beast on Earth.
Even the pirana only kill to eat.
Civilisation is a thin veneer
easily ruptured by hypnotists
to reveal the amoral life below,
as nightly they do on many a stage
for people's mindless entertainment.
So Hitler abused the German people.

And now we have the nuclear bomb.

Also on the Hai Lee, Kenneth Cook
who came aboard at Freetown,
one of two survivors of a crew of fifty
(twelve on the raft died off) sixty days
on a raft, kept a log on sail-cloth
(he later published a book about it).

34

Towards the end, the log is all of God,
God, God, God, pitiably clung to.
The U-boats made a religious of him.

For Thou dost mark the sparrow's fall.....

'Enry Capes liked his pint with the lads
and a game of darts at the local.
Dying of gangrene on the banks of the Chindwin,
mumbles deliriously a song:
> *I wonder who's kissing her now.*
> *I wonder who's teaching her how.*
> *I wonder if she*
> *Ever thinks about me.*
> *I wonder who's fuckin' her now.*

Czeslaw hunted in the Warsaw sewers
gets the first German with a stab to the chest,
but the second shoots him in the guts,
drowns in that river of piss and shit.

War is a filthy business.

So it drags on, deeps beneath Dante's musing —
Old Leather-Chops, dried in the fires of Hell.

To Arbela, Darius brought a million men,
but to Alexander they were one man — Darius.
He sent detachments to harass right and left
but himself charged straight for the centre — Darius,
who was saved by a bodyguard throwing himself
on Alexander's lance: but he fled the field.
The headless million was useless.

One stone in the brain killed all of Goliath.

Wars are not waged by peoples
but by chess-playing governors WITH peoples,
at once their weapons and their victims.
There'd be no wars if governors fought each other
instead of using their peoples.

Hostias et preces tibi, O Shiva.

> **The fathers fight each other
> to the last drop of the sons' blood,
> then call a truce among themselves
> till more sons are bred up for carnage.**

Agnus Dei, qui tollis peccata patri.

Young Hank, raised around Walden,
knew those oak-trees every one,
was a very promising flautist.
On Iwo-Jima he struggled up
the lava slopes of Suribachi,

bleak and dour, to find the Japs
dug in, almost impregnable,
and himself dying, in glazed horror
staring at his own guts spilled on the rock.

    Mr. Kagawa, a decent shipping clerk
in Nagoya, is known as a gentleman,
kindly, polite, deferential,
a good husband, father, neighbour,
trustworthy and competent.
In Hong Kong, Mr. Kagawa
helps to bayonet the patients
in a field hospital, helps to dismember
a hundred or so hospital staff,
slices off ears, cuts out tongues,
stabs out eyes, bayonets to death.
He helps to make beds of corpses
on which stripped and screaming nurses —
a Nellie Burns of Dundee among them —
are tied and raped by Mr. Kagawa
and his colleagues, then bayoneted.

    Just an old Bushido custom?

    And Ludwig Ramdohr of Ravensbruck,
sentenced to be hanged as a torturer,
merciless sadist and murderer,
was known to his friends of former days
as 'dear kind Ludwig', a man who couldn't
harm a fly or a bird or beast —
a sort of Schweitzer Reverer of Life.

    Sentimentality masks the brute?
or maybe people are just not animals.

Not Attila nor Jenghiz Khan
surpassed the atrocities of the Nazis,
millions carried off as slaves,
innocent people mass-murdered,
trades unionists, democrats, gypsies and homosexuals,
prisoners and hostages slain by the thousand,
ghettos gutted, their populations
carried in death-trains to murder-camps,
towns and villages rased, their folk
massacred to the last child,
lands laid waste and desert,
all material wealth plundered
and carried off to Germany.
Peoples not held to be Teutonic
classed as sub-human.

Freude, schoner Gotterfunken......
Alle Menschen werden bruder......

40

The monster Heydrich slain by Czech partisans,
the Germans descend on Lidice,
shoot all the men and some of the women,
take others off to Ravensbruck
where many die of vicious abuse,
new-born babies are murdered,
all children taken from mothers —
nine-year-old Emmy from Sophie among them.
None is ever heard of again.
The village is then completely destroyed,
Sternbeck the priest tortured and shot
for refusing to renounce his flock.

In another French village hiding Macqui,
farmer Yves is murdered, Jeanne raped
and murdered, and little Jean, aged three,
tortured, then crucified on the gate.

And a little child shall lead them......

In Tavaux-in-Aine the Germans storm
the home of Macqui Moujeon, wound
his wife, break her arms and legs, pour
petrol on her and burn her alive,
all in front of the five children
who then are locked in the cellar, the house
set fire to, but put out in time by neighbours.

In Oradour-sur-Glane the Boche
sweep in, pack all the men in a barn
and shoot the lot, though five survive
to tell the story, when the barn is fired.
Young Roby for one escapes the flames.

The women and children are packed in the church,
bales of straw brought in and fired
to smoke them all to death.
A stampede breaks the vestry door
but the would-be escapers are gunned down.
Only Maman Rauffanche survives,
discovered wounded in the vicarage garden.
Six hundred die, men, women and bairns.

Roncevaux!   L'ombre du grand Roland
n'est donc pas consolee......
Dieu!   Que le son du cor est triste aux fonds des bois!

Remember Lidice and Oradour
Remember.

And the village Earth?
None will be left to remember,
               if........

42

Lo pianto stesso li pianger non lascia.....

Their very tears forbid their further weeping
and the sorrow thus imprisoned in their eyes
turns inward, making the anguish worse.......

As if so to imprison tears
Death has built himself a kingdom
and called it Concentration Camp,
a university of degradation
with many different colleges:
Auschwitz, Dachau, Ravensbruck, Treblinka,
Neuengamme and the rest.

Starvation, torture, mass-murder,
humiliation, filth, the New Order
of Hitler's German civilisation
deepen the depths of Hell itself,
not for sinners but innocent victims,
blacken medicine by obscene experiments.
Science itself defiled and debased
(Mengele)
stinking death-trains bring in their loads
of human oven-fodder, the air
full of the smell of roasting flesh,
everything of the least value taken
from the valueless lives before their destruction,
three million in Auschwitz alone.

ARBEIT MACHT FREI
being worked to death frees you from living.

The alternative?   The electric wire.

43

People sleep like negroes in slave ships
in the early days of the Americas,
ordure and vomit foul the air,
the stench enough to sicken a dog,
lice and bugs the constant familiars,
warders hardened German criminals
released from jail, specially trained,
and punished for weakness and leniency,
the goal destruction of body and soul.

Starvation makes cannibals of some
flesh cut from dead bodies
when the guards aren't looking.

You have not come to a sanitorium
Fritsch tells the new arrivals.
Indeed, no health or holiday camps
are they, but the nadir of evil,
human inhumanity to humans.

Deutschland, Deutschland, Uber alles,
Uber alles in der Welt......
    in depravity.

Poor Papa Haydn.

Ilse Koch, aesthete in Buchenwald,
has prisoners with tattooed skins
killed and makes their skins into lampshades.
And Buchenwald goes psychiatric:
like Jivaro tribesmen
they shrink human heads.

Odette hears the screams of women thrown
alive into crematorial ovens,
the opening and the shutting of the doors.

No end of horror
in this Age of Horror —
unless?
And no art can contain it.

Let us remember
not only the Jewish men and women
remember
but suffer also the little children.

In Rama
was there a voice heard
lamentation and great mourning,
Rachel weeping for her children
and would not be comforted......

Leah, with little Sol and Mischa
taken in her time to the 'showers'
petrified, ordered to hang up her rags,
hides the children among them, enters
the death chamber alone, praying

Boruch ate adonai elohaynu.......
Blessed art Thou, O Lord our God......
But the S.S. search the clothing
and, too far to reach them,
she sees them pushed in, the doors closed.

In Rama
      Rachel weeping
  but in Dachau
      Misery has outwept her tears.

Man's greatest passion, said Jung,
is indolence.   Would that it were.
Man's greatest passion is slaughtering people.

Better the world were fast asleep
Than kept awake by Mars.

The barbarians run mad in Poland,
unresisting villagers shot or burned,
their houses fired, grenaded, pillaged.
Old Wladek and Marshka in Pinczow
among three hundred dead,
burned alive for no kind reason
but policy: terrorising 'subhuman' Poles.
People are locked in their houses
the houses fired, escapers shot.

The German supermen have arrived.

Poland becomes a slave colony,
mass murder rampages, mass burials,
victims digging their own graves with bare hands.
Wladek Pietras sees Mum and Dad,
Granny, two brothers, three sisters,
and baby Terese burned alive.

Poland is to be cleared for German settlers.

Jews are forced to undress and jump
into mass-graves bottomed with quick-lime,
whole families, babies and all,
the graves flooded with water
and then filled in.

Non me lasciar cosi disfatto.......
Leave me not so undone.......

And people whispered of Messire Dante:
see there the man who has been to Hell.

In Russia, the same techniques and policy
with even viler barbarity,
layer on layer of people shot
and the bodies burned in layers of quicklime,
all done under orders, soldiers
deliberately debased and corrupted,
forced to find the stomach for it,
the wets who can't, replaced by special units
of men trained to have no qualms.
Hitler orders that nothing done to
Russians should be considered crime.
Rape, torture, the most vicious murders,
all are sanctioned against Russians.
They give special courses in ruthlessness.

Children are used for target practice,
baby Natasha, aged ten months,
pinned by bayonet to her dead mother's breast,
pregnant Olga is gang-raped,
then her lovers cut her throat.
Schoolgirls are carried off as sex-slaves,
those unwanted, and schoolboys, shot.
All the women of many a village
are raped, respectable matrons
forced into brothels for use by the troops,
women are often raped in public
their menfolk forced to witness it,
priests murdered if they intervene.

And yet God has not said a word.

Sonia, aged about sixteen
is taken from her mother and friends,
gang-raped, her breasts cut off,
nailed to a tree and left to die.

Die geliebte Mullerin ist mein, ist mein!

Whole populations are massacred,
herded into barns and burnt alive.
At Kiev fifty-two thousand people
of all ages and both sexes
tortured and murdered; at Rostow
many thousands done to death.
Dead Russians can't fight back.
Major Roesen can't stand it
and sends back a mass-murder report.

Officers freeze men to death in water-butts,
strangle folk with their own bare hands.

Ubermenschen.

Twelve million persons murdered,
two-thirds of Europe's Jews......

And the Russians are cruel to poor old Hess,
expensively kept alive in Spandau?

Hitler's iron chariots drowned
in a Red Sea of Russian blood.

49

The war in Europe uproars to its climax,
landings in Italy, Anzio beachhead
Cassino shattered, Mussolini arrested,
the Rhine crossed, the Russians in Vienna.

The Allies themselves contribute to
the atrocious history of war atrocities
with saturation bombing of civilian targets:
Berlin, Dresden know such horror
as London never did, for both sides
make unimaginable technical strides
in the dirty business of slaughtering people.
The German cities suffer more deaths
than Hiroshima and Nagasaki
because of the evil and untrue doctrine
that rulers can be defeated
by massacring their peoples.
The Blitz alone gave that the lie.

Under Badoglio the Italians change sides
and reap the wrath of their ex-partners.
No country lane the allies tread
driving the Germans up through Italy
and on through France and the Low Countries,
but a hard and gruelling pilgrimage
to plunge Hitler in his twilight of the gods.

But steadily the net tightens
round Berlin, the rope around her throat,
and deranged Hitler's wicked dreams
bring his world crashing down on his head.
The Red Army triumphant,
poised to take Berlin,
he blows his brains out.

Horror stalks Europe before
the unconditional surrender:
whole German divisions wiped out,
Caen obliterated before its recapture,
its civilian survivors meeting their rescuers
like dazed zombies the eye winces at,
their liberation worse than the occupation
which at least left them their town intact.

Countesses whore for a bar of soap,
cigarettes, a bite of food
for their children, their husbands, themselves.
Never in the history of prostitution
have so many women of such quality
so traded their bodies for so little,
so often, to so many.

> *Das Ewig-Weibliche*
> *Zieht uns hinan.*

Traded?   The victors can simply grab,
and maternity hospitals are raided,
women, pregnant, or newly delivered,
raped, their nurses also,
in the first mad days of invasion,
women from eight to eighty.

War is indeed a dirty business
especially for the weak and defenceless,
the women and children, the old and the sick.

Even after the killing is over
there is the mess, the reprisals to be taken,

collaborators and traitors to be dealt with,
women's heads to be shaved in public,
men to be shot, hanged, or battered to death.
And there are the liberated camps,
the chaos of the Displaced Persons.

Incredulity rules at first
as the liberators enter the camps
and see such sights
as Dante would have swooned at:
piles of naked corpses, mass graves,
living skeletons gaping,
women shrinking from the look in eyes
that wince at their degradation,
the wails of erupting, pent-up grief.

Ludmilla howls in solitary shame
till G.I. Rubinstein pulls her to him
and lets her, like a child, soak his shirt
with tears, holding her tight in arms
that tell her at last it is over,
she is safe again, back in the body
of humankind, hearing the language
only the body speaks, of union,
tenderness, comfort, love and acceptance,
the age-old wisdom of the flesh
that knows itself human, and knows no barrier
of race or colour, tongue or creed,
knows only the unity of humankind
beyond all divisions, beyond war itself,
the solidarity of the human species
in one destiny of evolution
that will triumph over all evil systems
as her brightest children inherit Mother Earth,

war a haunting nightmare of the past
like the tail we shed somewhere far back,
the russet fur, the simian gait and teeth.
And with war, the moral-aesthetic filth
of capitalist commercialism,
the spiritual sickness of our time.
Politics and economics will be again
matters of moral-aesthetic values
as Socrates, Plato, Aristotle knew them,
as the Prophets and other great and good men knew them.

The poetry the pity: the pity the understanding.

In Dachau GIs weep at the horror,
strong men, not specially good,
but real and human.
They round up the German guards
and stand them against a wall,
their arrogant commander with them —
an arrogance only saints might bear.
Mutters of rage from sickened GIs
grow in intensity and menace
till one American boy goes wild
and opens up with a machine-gun.
Encouraged by shouts of 'Kill them all',
his own officer poker-faced,
he does just that:
'all' is a hundred and twenty-two.
Among the dead is Irma's Rudi.

Dulc' et decorum est......
Douce, most fitting it is to die for the Fatherland.

The war in Europe is now over,
the revolution has won vast ground,
the good society is nearer hand,
Tito's triumph somehow symbolic
as the Yugoslavs free themselves.

But the Greek socialists, trying to choose
the freedom won by the Yugoslavs
are robbed of it by an enemy
as bad, to them, as Hitler.
Winston Churchill uses the British Army
to restore the vicious old regime
which leads to the reign of the fascist colonels:

all the result of a cynical carve-up
of other nations' lands and futures
by Churchill and Stalin at Yalta.

Not for Hirihito, Hitler's end.
The emperor makes others do his dying,
lose his face, pay for his crimes.

Hirohito knew he had lost the war
by January nineteen forty-four,
but refused to sue for peace.
If Japan was not to have an empire,
there must be fewer Japanese,
and enemy troops could best achieve that.
Also, the greater the defeat
the more the people suffer
and the easier it is to sell surrender
to a people trained to prefer death:
the more compassion from friend and foe.
These and other motives make
the Emperor soldier on
for more than another year and a half,
losing another million lives
before the atom bomb gives him
the perfect excuse to end the war
before he himself is cooked in Tokyo,
the next atomic target.

Japanese peace-feelers there have been
for months before the bomb is dropped,
but the scientists have to test their toys,
so the cryptic feelers are ignored.
The Japanese get no real warning,
nor are the people themselves appealed to
by dropping warning leaflets among them.
The worst war-crime against civilians
(except Dresden?) is planned and set up.

But already the Americans
have burned twice as many citizens
of Tokyo and other cities
by saturation incendiary bombing
as die in Hiroshima and Nagasaki.

War has long ceased to be war
and become an orgy of mad destruction
not just between armies but whole populations,
waged by monstrous war-machines
controlled no more by their creators
to achieve ends that once seemed human.

Young Kunio is a studious boy,
not much use for soldiering
and therefore no great loss.
Taught some basic pilot-skills
he can aim a plane, loaded with bombs,
onto an aircraft-carrier deck,
and so he does, the white bandana
samurai wore when not intending
to survive a battle, round his head
to signify he has joined the Immortals
in kamikaze, the 'divine wind'.

Such tactics argue desperation.
With Kunio, the old Japan
crashed on the deck of the U.S. Navy.

The Japanese death-wish takes grizzly toll
of not only their but American lives
as they fight to the last dying breath
in inhuman pain and squalor,

the hara-kiri of a nation's army
torturing itself to death,
courage beyond reason a deadly sin.

The end comes after Nagasaki,
and MacArthur, taking the Emperor over
in the new gang-up against the Soviets,
is taken over by the shrewd Emperor,
as the G.Is. are by the Japanese people.

The scene is set to receive the victors:
middle-class women sent off to the hills,
the others encouraged to welcome them,
the officers by upper-class women
in diplomatic intercourse well-trained,
the other ranks by working-class girls.

**Defeated Japan conquers her conqueror,
receiving the victor with open legs.**

You and I again, Eve, have endured
the inhuman pain the seed of our innocent love
unleash upon the world and on themselves,
blaming it all on our alleged transgression.
We who have suffered every atrocious spasm:
we who have died with every violent death:
who suffer the pangs of being born again:
we the immortal spirit of mankind,
who rise again from the dead of each new war,
must bear again the animal flesh of life
and from the smoking ruins build the future.

Flowers grow on the broken wall
grass takes over the rubble mound,
bushes sprout on the burnt-out roof,
and in the sepulchres of ocean
forms of submarine life festoon
the sunken ships and aeroplanes:
crabs inhabit ribs and skulls,
fish through galley and porthole glide.
Life again takes over, Nature
herself recycles our destructiveness.

Blind hands learn to read,
legs no longer there contrive to stride,
the plough furrows the war-wasted soil,
New towns rise from the ruins of the old.
Enemies fate had destined for one grave
find themselves enraptured in one bed.
Once again our kind from nightmare wakens.
Once again illness is convalescent.
Once again we have survived our shame,
the obloquy of self-inficted wounds.

For how long?   Will tolerant Nature
let our kind survive still worse disgrace?
Or in final failure let her experiment end?
Begin again another evolution?
Or has the abyss of wickedness been sounded,
the slow climb from the pit at last begun?

Shall we yet see, in centuries to come,
that half-forgotten gate we came out from
so long ago, welcome the fallen home?

Shall we live to see love triumph over war?

Gaze on the spires of New Jerusalem?

THE BLEW BLANKET LIBRARY

The Blew (or Blue) Blanket was the privileged insignia of the craftsmen of Edinburgh in the time of James III. It was pledged to them by Privy Seal in 1482 when the craftsmen of the city, together with the merchants and other loyal subjects, marched on Edinburgh Castle and freed their King. It remained their insignia for centuries, and one of the original *Blew Blankets* is today in the Museum of Antiquities in Edinburgh.

The Blew Blanket Library is a collection of new books on Scotland by Scottish writers. Its aim is to provide a forum where writer-craftsmen of all types can display their wares in the context of Scotland today.

Already available in *The Blew Blanket Library*.

THE CROFTING YEARS. Francis Thompson.

A remarkable and moving study of crofting in the Highlands and Islands. It tells of the bloody conflicts a century ago when the crofters and their families faced all the forces of law and order and demanded a legal status and security of tenure, and of how gunboats cruised the Western Isles in Government's classic answer.

Life in the crofting townships is described with great insight and affection. Food, housing, healing and song are all dealt with. But the book is no nostalgic longing for the past. It looks to the future and argues that crofting must be carefully nurtured as a reservoir of potential strength for an uncertain future.

Francis Thompson lives and works in Stornoway. His life has been intimately bound up with the crofters, and he well knows of what he writes.

ISBN 0 946487 06 5. Paperback Price: £3:00p.

TALL TALES FROM AN ISLAND. Peter Macnab.

These tales come from the island of Mull, but they could just as well come from anywhere in the Highlands or Islands.

Witches, ghosts, warlocks and fairies abound, as do stories of the people, their quiet humour and their abiding wit. A book to dip into, laugh over and enthuse about. Out of this great range of stories a general picture appears of an island people, stubborn and strong in adversity, but warm and co-operative and totally wedded to their island way of life. It is a clear picture of a microcosmic society perfectly adapted to an environment that, in spite of its great beauty, can be harsh and unforgiving.

Peter Macnab was born and grew up on Mull, and he knows and loves every inch of it. Not for him the 'superiority' of the incomer who makes joke cardboard figures of the island people and their ways. He presents a rounded account of Mull and its people.

ISBN 0 946487. Paperback. Price: £3:95p.

THE EDGE OF THE WOOD. Alan Bold.

This is Alan Bold's first solo collection of short stories, and it is an impressive one. Here we have tales of the Scottish reality of today, tales told by a master craftsman. It is a fine collection, ranging from murder in a Scottish village to a Black Hole in Space, from a man's love for his dog to a young poet's first love and first poem. One of Scotland's foremost writers of today, Alan Bold has produced a collection of short stories which illustrate, through the eye of an artist, many of Scotland's current problems and contradictions.

ISBN 0 946487 08 1. Paperback. Price £4:25p

THE JOLLY BEGGARS OR LOVE AND LIBERTY.

Robert Burns. A facsimile of the original handwritten copy by Burns himself, with the poet's corrections.

This unusual volume contains not only the original text, but also the printed text on facing pages, and another text with glossary. It contains all the songs and music, and they are newly illustrated by John Hampson, a young Scottish artist of great promise. There is a long Introduction by Tom Atkinson, and an Essay on *Poetry, Politics and Forgetfulness* by William Neil, himself a poet of South-west Scotland. Although but little known today, *Love and Liberty* contains some of Robert Burns's most brilliant poetry and most lively songs. It was Scotland's poet at the height of his genius and power.

This Volume should certainly be on the shelves of every lover of Robert Burns.

ISBN 0 946487 02 2. Casebound. Price £8:00p.

WILD PLACES. William Neill.

Publication of these new poems and broadsheets by William Neill marks a very important step in contemporary Scottish letters. Writing in English, Scots and Gaelic, and translating between them, William Neill brings a strongly disciplined vision to bear on his native land. The lyricism and freedom of his language is matched by the beauty of his imagery, and to that imagery he brings the fruit of Scotland's. three linguistic cultures. From such a synthesis has sprung poetry of a strength and virility rarely matched.

Wild Places received a Scottish Arts Council Award on publication, in recognition of its high standard.

ISBN 0 946487 11 1. Paperback. £5:00p

LUATH PRESS GUIDES TO WESTERN SCOTLAND

SOUTH WEST SCOTLAND. Tom Atkinson.

A guidebook to the best of Kyle, Carrick, Galloway, Dumfriesshire, Kirkcudbrightshire and Wigtownshire.

This lovely land of hills, moors and beaches is bounded by the Atlantic and the Solway. Steeped in history and legend, still unspoiled, it is a land whose peace and grandeur are at least comparable to the Highlands.

Legends, history and loving descriptions by a local author make this an essential book for all who visit — or live in — the country of Robert Burns.

ISBN 0 946847 04 9. Paperback. £2:00p.

THE LONELY LANDS. Tom Atkinson.

A guide book to Inveraray, Kintyre, Glen Coe, Loch Awe, Loch Lomond, Cowal, the Kyles of Bute, and all of central Argyll.

All the glories of Argyll are described in this book. From Dumbarton to Campbeltown there is a great wealth of beauty. It is a a quiet and lonely land, a land of history and legend, a land of unsurpassed glory.

Tom Atkinson describes it all, writing with deep insight of the land he loves. There could be no better guide to its beauties and history. Every visitor to this country of mountains and lochs and lonely beaches will find that enjoyment is enhanced by reading this book.

ISBN 0 946847 10 3. Paperback. Price: £2:00p.

ROADS TO THE ISLES. Tom Atkinson. A guidebook to Scotland's Far West, including Morar, Moidart, Morvern and Ardnamurchan.

This is the area lying to the west and north-west of Fort William. It is a land of still unspoiled loveliness, of mountain, loch and silver sands. It is a vast, quiet land of peace and grandeur. Legend, history and vivid description by an author who loves the area and knows it intimately make this book essential to all who visit this Highland wonderland.

ISBN 0 946487 01 4. Paperback. £1:80p.

THE EMPTY LANDS   Tom Atkinson.

A guidebook to the north-west of Scotland, from Fort William to Cape Wrath, and from Bettyhill to Lairg.

This is the fourth book in the series *Guides to Western Scotland*, and it covers that vast empty quarter leading up to Cape Wrath. These are the Highlands of myth and legend, a land of unsurpassed beauty where sea and mountain mingle in majesty and grandeur. As in his other books, the author is not content to describe the scenery (which is really beyond description), or advise you where to go. He does all of that with his usual skill and enthusiasm, but he also places that superb landscape into its historical context, and tells how it and the people who live there have become what we see today. With love and compassion, and some anger, he has written a book which should be read by everyone who visits or lives in — or even dreams about — that empty land.

ISBN 0 946487 13 8.   Price £2:50p.

ALSO FROM LUATH PRESS.

WALKS IN THE CAIRNGORMS.   Ernest Cross.

The Cairngorms are the highest uplands in Britain, and walking there introduces you to sub-arctic scenery found nowhere else. This book provides a selection of walks in a splendid and magnificent countryside — there are rare birds, animals and plants, geological curiosities, quiet woodland walks, unusual excursions in the mountains.

Ernest Cross has written an excellent guidebook to these things. Not only does he have an intimate knowledge of what he describes, but he loves it all deeply, and this shows.

ISBN 0 946487 09 X   Paperback.   £1:80p

THE SCOT AND HIS OATS.   G.W. Lockhart.

A survey of the part played by oats and oatmeal in Scottish history, legend, romance and the Scottish character.

Sowing and mowing, stooking and stacking, milling and cooking, they are all in this book. Wallace Lockhart's research has carried him from Froissart to Macdiarmid, and his recipes range from an oatmeal *aperitif* to oatmeal candy. His stories about oats traverse the world from Mafeking to Toronto.

ISBN 0 946487 05 7.   Paperback.   Price £1:80p.

POEMS TO BE READ ALOUD: *A Victorian Drawing Room Entertainment.* Selected and with an Introduction by Tom Atkinson.

A very personal selection of poems specially designed for all those who believe that the world is full of people who long to hear you declaim such as these. The Entertainment ranges from an unusual and beautiful *Love Song* translated from the Sanskrit, to the drama of *The Shooting of Dan McGrew* and *The Green Eye of the Little Yellow God,* to the bathos of *Trees* and the outrageous bawdiness of *Eskimo Nell.* Altogether, a most unusual and amusing selection.

ISBN 0 946487 00 6. Paperback. Price £1:80p.

HIGHLAND BALLS AND VILLAGE HALLS
G.W. Lockhart.

There is no doubt about Wallace Lockhart's love of Scottish country dancing, nor of his profound knowledge of it. Reminiscence, anecdotes, social comment and Scottish history, tartan and dress, prose and verse, the steps of the most important dances — they are are all brought together to remind, amuse and instruct the reader in all facets of Scottish country dancing. Wallace Lockhart practices what he preaches. He grew up in a house where the carpet was constantly being lifted for dancing, and the strains of country dance music have thrilled him in castle and village hall. He is the leader of the well-known *Quern Players*, and he composed the dance *Eilidh MacIain*, which was the winning jig in the competition held by the Edinburgh Branch of the Royal Scottish Country Dance Society to commemorate its sixtieth anniversary.

This is a book for all who dance or who remember their dancing days. It is a book for all Scots.

ISBN 0 946487 12 X. Price: £3:75p.

Any of these books can be obtained from your bookseller, or, in case of difficulty, please send price shown, plus 30p. for post and packing to:-

**LUATH PRESS Ltd.,
Barr, Ayrshire, KA 26 9TN. U.K.**